COLLATERAL DAMAGE: WHEN WHAT HAPPENED *SPIRITUALLY* WAS YOUR FAULT by Dr. Marlene Miles

Freshwater Press 2025

Freshwaterpress9@gmail.com

ISBN: 978-1-967860-97-5

Paperback Version

Table of Contents

COLLATERAL DAMAGE

When What Happened Spiritually Was Your Fault

Freshwater

Collateral Damage

When the Spirit of the Lord moves upon you, you must not quench it. You must listen, heed, and do what the Spirit says. Sometimes the Spirit may tell you not to go a particular place at a particular time or even with a particular person. Did you listen? Or did you go anyway? And did you feel at that time that nothing seemed to happen?

Okay, good.

If you are one who has been through spiritual attacks, you may not have known when the attack really started. Perhaps it was only felt when it became heavy or oppressive; but that may not have been when it really started. It may have had its genesis the night you went to that certain place with a certain person when the Holy Spirit told you not to go.

But something did happen and may still be happening, yet you may not know its source. Until you know if you are under witchcraft or other occultic attack, you may think that uncomfortable events, oppressive events, losses, disappointments and afflictions can be explained away as, *'that's the way life is.'* But it may not be that; it could be something else, entirely.

Now, we can't always blame everything on someone else, but there may be times that things happen to us because of being in the wrong place at the wrong time. I think of terror events in public places. The terrorist may have been targeting everyone or as many as possible. But in some cases, an active shooter, for example, may have been after one person. The rest may be hurt or fall and be called collateral damage. If only they hadn't been in that place at that particular time--, *right*?

Collateral damage means unintended harm or destruction that occurs as a side effect of a deliberate action. This could be in military, political, economic, or even social contexts. The term is often used to refer to civilian casualties, property loss, or environmental destruction that happen while pursuing a legitimate target or goal. But, it could also be in spiritual contexts. We've seen our share of fallen pastors, for example. Yes, they may have done wrong. Yes, they may have fallen, they may have victimized one or more people, in or out of the congregation. But, spiritually, in the congregation, whatever that pastor was, he released it over the congregation, through the mic, through the laying on of hands. Whatever his doctrine was also became the doctrine of the congregants who sat in the pews or in those chairs, either suddenly or over time. Whatever *spirits* he carried were also released over that group.

If only you hadn't have sat under that pastor. If only you had never let him lay hands on you in prayer. If *only...*

A church installed a pastor who was a womanizer. All of a sudden, many men in the church wanted to divorce their wives. There you go. That lustful, eye-roaming, unfaithful *spirit* was released over the congregation although the pastor may have been hiding it and may have looked upright the entire time, well, at least through the interview process. That is collateral damage. The *spirits* that the pastor harbored knew that if they struck the shepherd, the sheep would scatter. Warfare against pastors is keen, so be sure to pray for your spiritual leaders.

Collateral damage happens when an action designed to achieve one goal has secondary, negative consequences that were not the direct intention, but were foreseeable or inevitable. No one would ever think that going to church could be damaging to them, in any way--, but in this case it happened. This is worse with satanic or occultic pastors who hide who they really are and are really initiating or nominating their congregants for evil.

That's not a mistake to the one doing the nominating, but it is surprise damage or destruction to the regular person on the pew.

Collateral damage is when a strike hits its intended target but also damages nearby people or property. Collateral damage may be when a pastor, prophet or teacher just says anything for popularity or to get clicks, attention, fame, or money--, but what they are sharing is false or heretical. This will damage or even destroy a mind or soul. That avid "minister" may just be trying to hit the wallets of the congregants, but their souls end up in captivity, sold, or destroyed. This is why ministry is nothing to play around with.

In a military context we may see civilian deaths or injuries, Destruction of non-military property, Disruption of essential services such as water, electricity, hospitals.

In medical advances we may see a good result for a certain disease or symptom, but there may be crazy side effects.

Even so, collateral damage is often unavoidable when weapons are used near populated areas or when intelligence is imperfect. When something goes awry, don't we hear this lamentation more often than we want to that 'it wasn't supposed to go this far'?

Across all contexts, collateral damage usually involves unintended victims, unintended impact on people or property, and often long-term consequences, social, psychological, emotional, mental, physical, and spiritual.

The man who thinks he is hiding his sin but has a public platform is spreading destruction wherever he goes. If he doesn't even have a platform, he can be destructive in small circles with whomever he interacts with, marries, dates or forms alliances with. He is also spreading destruction to his offspring. It's only a matter of time.

Biblical Collateral Damage

Collateral damage in the Bible, meaning unintended suffering, destruction, or consequences that occurred as a result of divine judgment, human sin, or military action.

The Bible doesn't use the modern phrase *collateral damage*, the concept appears often throughout its pages and it's one of the reasons I wrote this book. This type of damage is when innocent or uninvolved people experience harm as a result of another person's sin, a nation's disobedience, or a larger divine or military event. It is when one person's sin brings suffering to others.

Many biblical stories show how one person's wrongdoing causes pain to others—sometimes whole families or nations. I will mention him again, but for now, Achan (Joshua 7) secretly took forbidden plunder from Jericho. Because of his disobedience, Israel lost its next battle at Ai, and many innocent soldiers died. *Collateral damage:* The deaths of the soldiers and the eventual execution of Achan's family and livestock.

David's Census (2 Samuel 24) King David ordered a census out of pride, against God's will. As punishment, a plague killed 70,000 Israelites. *Collateral damage:* Ordinary citizens suffered for their king's sin.

Jonah's Disobedience (Jonah 1) Jonah fled from God's command, causing a violent storm that endangered the sailors on his ship. *Collateral damage:* The sailors nearly died because of Jonah's personal rebellion. Not only that, the entire ship, not as valuable as the lives of the men, but still pricey, was lost.

Sometimes God's judgments or purifications of sin involve widespread consequences, such as the Flood (Genesis 6–9).

Sodom and Gomorrah (Genesis 19) were destroyed for their wickedness, yet everyone in the area perished except Lot and his daughters. Even Lot's wife died when she looked back. c*ollateral damage:* Innocent bystanders, homes, animals, and land destroyed.

Egyptian Plagues (Exodus 7–12): Pharaoh's hardness of heart led to national suffering. Plagues released included frogs, boils, hail, darkness, and death of the firstborn. *Collateral damage:* Egyptian civilians endured suffering because of Pharaoh's refusal.

The Bible presents collateral damage as part of a moral tension between justice and mercy. Sometimes, harm to others reveals the corporate nature of sin. One person's rebellion can spread through families and nations. Prophets such as Ezekiel and Jeremiah emphasize that God takes no pleasure in the death of the wicked, suggesting such events are tragic, not arbitrary.

Jesus' teachings reframe this by urging compassion and forgiveness, warning that sin and hardness of heart still produce unintended harm (Matthew 5–7, Luke 13:1–5).

Watchman

But if the watchman see the sword come, and blow not the trumpet, and the people be not warned; if the sword come, and take any person from among them, he is taken away in his iniquity; but his blood will I require at the watchman's hand. (Ezekiel 33:6)

This book is about the above verse, but it is about so much more than that. Yes, when the Lord shows you something and you are to tell people and you don't, when something happens to them, that means their blood will be on your hands. However, as a watchman on the wall, the job is intercession, and that means to pray for others as the Lord assigns you. in this very real way, something could happen to another or others if the intercessor, for example is not interceding.

The pastor, is the shepherd, and may serve as watchman. The husband is as the pastor of his home. The intercessor or prophet who sees but doesn't warn is causing damage and destruction to him or herself, as well as to those he should be watching out for. If you are called as a watchman, but your mouth has been bridled by a legal authority over you; then that person will pay for not letting you tell what God said to who God said to tell it to. It seems from Isaiah 6:1 that the Prophet Isaiah 'didn't see the Lord' until King Uzziah died.

In the Bible we see other examples of willful disobedience that caused harm or even death to other people.

Diana went out to see the daughters of the land (Genesis) that resulted in an entire city of men being slaughtered and the women and children of that city being captured and taken to become slaves. The wickedness of a person's sin is great, but the iniquity is even greater. The iniquity lasts and lasts, even into the third and fourth generations. It's why we pray and ask the Lord to remove our iniquity, the iniquity of our bloodline, or of our city or nation. Amen.

I learned from a plumbing leak in my home that the water bill from the leak can be high, but the bill is even higher than just the cost of the water because the fee for the sewage to drain the leaking water is greater than the water usage itself. If we say the leak is the sin, then the sewage is the iniquity of that sin. It costs a great deal to be rid of iniquity. It takes at least repentance, prayer, fasting, spiritual warfare, and God's forgiveness.

Achan stole spoils and stored them in his tent; he and his whole family were stoned and burned. When something like that happens and the person knows they are putting danger or damnation in their own life as well as all around him, or with him that is the same as a suicide bomber, for example. It is not always accidental sin. Sometimes people don't know how dangerous they are, or how dangerous their choices are, or that they are in danger at all. Built into sin is the idea that the sinner or perpetrator will get away with it --, else they wouldn't do it. The fact that Achan hid the items meant that he planned to get away with it and use the items later.

Jonah didn't steal anything; he just stole away from Ninevah by going in the very opposite direction on a ship bound for Tarshish. The entire ship was lost. Ships don't just sail themselves; there's a whole crew on the vessel as well as any other passengers. Jonah involved all of these people in his rebellion, in his sin. Jonah may have had no idea that his actions might harm others. There was heavy collateral damage due to Jonah's disobedience.

Hezekiah showed the envoy from Babylon all that was in his store and treasury. Later the entire kingdom was captured and taken away to Babylon. (Isaiah 6)

Aaron listened to the people and built a golden calf for them to idolize. This made God to repent of these people, and they wandered in the wilderness for 40 years and never got into the Promised Land. Millions of people died in the Wilderness; their descendants got in, but not them.

Rachel stole her father's idols when they left Laban's ranch. Rachel ended up dying in childbirth and Jacob suffered loss of Joseph, thinking he was dead for 17 years when Joseph had been sold as a slave into Egypt.

General idolatry in the kingdoms of Israel got them captured again and taken into bondage in Babylon.

The foolish Galatians suffered general captivity by Simon the Sorcerer because the people of Galatia didn't know any better and didn't discern and may not have fought against idolatry, so they were dragged into legalism. These people were in captivity. But they were still walking around and living their lives. They may have been walking around, but if they are not living the life that God sent them here to live, then they are living another whole life. A programmed life. An unseen life. Captivity.

O foolish Galatians, who hath bewitched you, that ye should not obey the truth, before whose eyes Jesus Christ hath been evidently set forth, crucified among you?
(Galatians 3:1)

Any of us can think of the times that we ourselves or someone we may know may have disregarded or disobeyed a word from the Lord. In that case, that one may have suffered. If others suffered, whether a few, or many people, that was collateral damage.

Collateral damage is not just now, it can extend into the future. For instance, a nuclear explosion. The blast may hurt a lot of people, but the radioactive fallout is there for generations – kind of like iniquity.

If because of that iniquity leading people into afflictions and more sin and down evil timelines, it could be that a person who should have been a pastor, never became a pastor. If an intercessor never interceded. If a prophet never prophesied, if a teacher never taught, or if an evangelist never witnessed to the lost. If these are the people, per chance that were lost in the hypothetical blast or were affected by the radiation after the nuclear explosion, that is far reaching iniquity. That is collateral damage to the original blast. That is cause with resultant, latent effects.

Especially judged if spiritual damage is committed or allowed, will be the fivefold ministry gifts. Pastors who are hirelings and not pastors at all; teachers will be judged more harshly. As well, lying prophets will suffer tremendously. Those who prophesy lightly instead of saying what thus saith the Lord. Any of those gifts who have watch over that house will be judged differently than laypeople.

Adam didn't do what God said, but did what Eve said, which was what the Serpent said. All of mankind was collateral damage and we were all under the Curse of the Law until Jesus came to redeem us.

And they said unto Moses, Because *there were* no graves in Egypt, hast thou taken us away to die in the wilderness? wherefore hast thou dealt thus with us, to carry us forth out of Egypt?" (Exodus 14:11)

In the Wilderness, in their murmuring and complaining, the Israelites got what they said. It may take a confluence of unfortunate events to create another unfortunate outcome. Was Moses the sole cause of them not reaching the Promised Land? Or was it a few? It could have been only one:

Wisdom *is* better than weapons of war: but one sinner destroyeth much good.
(Ecclesiastes 9:18)

In the Wilderness, the people were rebellious, idolatrous, disobedient, murmuring and complaining and God hated it. They contributed to not getting into the Promised Land.

Moses did have his part though. Moses' was disobedient also. Even though Moses led faithfully for decades, *he himself* was later forbidden to enter the land. (Numbers 20:1–13)

At Meribah, the people once again complained of thirst. God told Moses to speak to the rock so water would flow. Instead, Moses struck the rock twice in anger and said, "Must we bring you water out of this rock?"

God called this an act of unbelief and misrepresentation, saying Moses did not uphold Him as holy before the people.

God then decreed:

"Because you did not trust in Me enough to honor Me as holy in the sight of the Israelites, you will not bring this

community into the land I give them."
(Numbers 20:12, NIV)

Just to clarify: Moses' exclusion was a problem of personal discipline. It was a consequence of misrepresenting God's holiness, not the reason the people as a whole were excluded.

Individual Sin

There was another young man that I knew, and we took a road trip one day. When we reached our destination at or near a beach and had spent the day, we were either walking along, just when we got into a taxi. I recall, in the back of that taxi, we were seated together and there was a wallet, a man's wallet. I announced that we must go to the police station and turn it in. He said, "Why?" I let him convince me to keep it and divide what was in it. What did I want to do that for? To seem cool? To be on the same page with him because I thought our relationship might turn into something else? I knew better.

1. Lord, forgive me that transgression, in the Name of Jesus.

Some months later this young man had what seemed like a simple fender bender car accident. It made him disabled from doing the job that he had trained and studied for years to do. I thought he was being dramatic, even overly dramatic. I was skeptical. Some weeks after that, in another city, nowhere near him, I had the SAME accident, with the same injuries.

What did we have in common? The wallet. I believe that keeping the contents of the wallet was the source of the iniquity to allow the punishment that we both experienced. But was that all?

No. Saints of God do not pick up everything you see, even if it looks valuable. Even if it is money. Accursed things can be placed along the way, even in your own path. Remember monitoring *spirits* have followed you. They know your usual paths, they know what you are likely to do. You could be down in cash flow because the devil made that happen and there is a hundred-dollar bill on the ground right in front of you. Really?

2. Pray first. Lord, do I pick this up?

Witches, warlocks, wizards, sorcerers, those types of people can enchant even money. Even food. Even objects. You don't accept gifts from everyone, and you certainly don't eat everyone's food. Perhaps you shouldn't eat anyone's food. That very wallet could have been placed in our path, and we fell for it. Neither of us needed that money that was in the wallet. So, we are not free of sin until awareness of sin and repentance. **<u>Do not steal.</u>**

Was that all?

Oh, no. There was still more.

Unbeknownst to me, this fellow had a whole girlfriend or almost ex-fiancé whose father he had enraged because he wouldn't sign the prenup. I never met her, never met her people and don't know who they were in the natural or spiritually. But I did learn that they were financially affluent in the city they lived in. In my spirit it feels like retribution, payback for what he did to this girl.

But why did it also happen to me?

I was collateral damage and never should have been with this guy who was betrothed to someone else. I never should have been talked into keeping even a dollar from that wallet. I knew better, but didn't do better.

Ancestral Sin

Most obvious in collateral damage is generational or ancestral sin. It is the iniquity of that sin that follows into the third and fourth generations and even beyond that causes man to suffer for something his ancestors did. Iniquity is the smoke from the fire of whatever your ancestors did. I've counted them--, your ancestors. If we are talking about the 4th generation there are 32 people who could have affected your life even now, years and years ago by leaving iniquity in the foundation of your bloodline. That's 32 people who could have committed one sin, or several sins, or many sins, many times and not repented for any of it. Your folks could have been completely reprobate for all you know. *Yikes.*

Yup. Yikes.

When you are afflicted or feel you are afflicted and you know that you know that you didn't do anything, suspect ancestral sin. We can call that collateral damage because what sinner is thinking about their children? But they should be. What sinner is thinking about their grandchildren? What sinner is thinking about their great grandkids? Most sinners think that sin is an individual choice, they mistakenly think that it is an individual transaction, it is for now and that there will be no repercussions from it.

They think, 'this is not hurting anyone.' They further think, or do not think that it will live on and it can hurt everything, and that it carries the iniquity of that very sin and transgression. Well, all of that is certainly false. But we will pray later on about being victims of this kind of collateral damage.

Corporate Sin

When the whole group sins--, even if they vote on it and reach a consensus, if it is not what God said, either by His Word, or expressly as a proceeding or prophetic word, then it is still sin. Sin has iniquity. Sin leads to death but on the way, there is affliction, there is pain, there is sorrow, there is loss, poverty, sickness, disappointment – and etcetera.

You want to live in paradise? You want to move to a certain place… what is the spiritual condition of that place, that state, that nation, that island--, those people? Is that city very sinful? Whatever befalls that city when you are there or live there, you may be a victim of collateral damage.

A corrupt political leader spreads his *spirits* throughout his jurisdiction. Those in authority usher in Grace or judgment, depending on who they are to God.

A corrupt pastor, for example can spread whatever is in him or her across an entire congregation. Just because a pastor dresses well, looks good, sounds good, and even speaks the Word of God, doesn't mean he is of God and that he is living upright before the Lord. After all, the devil and his demons know the Bible. So, this pastor? How is he living? What is his real fruit? Else, his collection of *spirits* could bring an entire congregation down.

For example, there is one pastor who was so excited to meet his future wife, and they felt a connection because they both had 11:11 tattoos. Folks, eleven-eleven is a divination designation. A person would have to be pretty deep into it to actually TATTOO it on their body.

Divination is sin. When the leader sins, it is as though the entire congregation also sins. Collateral damage is a real possibility here for many reasons. One, just stated, two the regularity of your attendance there. Presenting yourself at an altar is worship and with regularity, that is called religion. And three: You put money there? That is worship. You are locked in with that collective, so collective captivity, damage, loss, oppression, whatever is the result coming from that altar and the one priesting at that altar is a real possibility in your life.

I have said more than once about more than one place designated as a church that I have to put on the whole armor of God just to go in there. That's when I usually know that it is time to leave that church. Of course, I diligently seek the Lord before doing such a thing. I was at a wrong church for so long, I had to call a friend to pray with me, to pray me in to going to church there Sunday after Sunday. We'd usually start when the car started and pray me all the way into the parking lot. Lord, have Mercy!

There is a sure standard that people who lead others or teach others must reach, aspire to, and sustain. For example, I teach, write, speak, pray—I can't live just any kind of way. I have to walk upright before the Lord, as much as it is in me, by help of the Holy Spirit. If I fall, then I must repent quickly, else whatever *spirits* I allow in my life can be loosed in my writing, teaching, preaching, speaking, and praying. The same is true for all of us. If you have kids and you are the leader of your house, the same truth applies. Like shedding cells, it's automatic. Whatever is in your or on you will be left in your wake.

11:11

I really had not planned to talk about this in this book, but here we go. 11:11 is a numerology or New Age symbol, and to have it tattooed on one's body is beyond what the Bible says.

Ye shall not make any cuttings in your flesh for the dead, nor print any marks upon you: I am the LORD. (Leviticus 19:28)

God says about Himself in the Word:

Indeed, I have inscribed [a picture of] you on the palms *of My hands*;
Your city walls [Zion] are continually before Me. (Isaiah 49:16 AMP)

Inscribed, is engraved or graven. The Bible says we are to have no engraved (engraven) images. So, it's popular? If you were tattooed before salvation that is one thing, but once we accept Christ, we should study to show ourselves approved and know what the Bible says.

Back to the subject of this "engraving." The metaphysical meaning for many people is that repeatedly seeing 11:11 such as on clocks, receipts, etcetera is a *spiritual sign*. Common interpretations include: Awakening or alignment: You're becoming more spiritually aware or "in tune" with the universe.

Folks, I used to have a lot of dreams, because I did, I thought I was deep or spiritual. I didn't even know what the dreams meant at the time. So just because a thing is spiritual doesn't mean it is good. It could be bad. We have to study to show ourselves approved.

Other metaphysical beliefs regarding 11:11 include manifestation window: A moment when your thoughts are said to manifest quickly, so you're encouraged to focus on what you want.

Finally, but maybe the most popular is that 11:11 is an Angel number. In numerology, 11 is considered a "master number," associated with intuition, enlightenment, and higher purpose. Seeing it doubled, 11:11 is often called an "angel message" allegedly reminding you that you're on the right path.

Angel numbers numerology is divination.

Alternately a few Bible verses are often linked to 11:11 and I will tell people sometimes draw from them symbolically or prophetically. Before I list them, be reminded:

My son, keep thy father's commandment, and forsake not the law of thy mother.

Bind them continually upon thine heart, and tie them about thy neck.

When thou goest, it shall lead thee; when thou sleepest, it shall keep thee; when

thou awakest, it shall talk with thee.
(Proverbs 6:20-22)

Writing things on your heart, means that you learn and keep the Word there. It doesn't literally mean to write. If it did, wouldn't there be tattoo priests at church? And wouldn't it be free? Why would you go to a dark someplace in the middle of the night, drunk or high and do something like this on a dare? And with what motivation? To be pretty? To be different? To "tie" yourself to whomever you are inscribing on your skin? What inebriated person decides to go to a tattoo parlor to get a tattoo to glorify God? Don't come at me about this; I read about tattoos in the Bible.

When devils, demons and unclean *spirits* see certain markings on a person or on a person's house they are drawn to it. It attracts them. They say, 'That is our mark, that one is inviting us, or that one belongs to us. Let's go.' And then suddenly there is an influx of oppressive *spirits* in a person's life.

Worse, they are invited, so how can deliverance be easy from that?

But if you want to justify 11:11 with Scriptures, here are three:

But the land you are crossing the Jordan to take possession of is a land of mountains and valleys that drinks rain from heaven. (Deuteronomy 11:11)

Symbolically, many believers interpret this as entering into a *new season* or *promised place* that is sustained by God, not by human effort. *Rain from heaven* represents divine provision and blessing. Perhaps when people see 11:11, they sometimes view it as a reminder that *God Himself is the source* of what will nourish their next chapter.

Everything about that verse and its symbolism is true, but God did not say write it on your flesh, and especially not just the numbers. Just the numbers by themselves mean something else entirely.

And by faith even Sarah, who was past childbearing age, was enabled to bear

children because she considered Him
faithful who had made the
promise.(Hebrews 11:11)

This verse points to *faith in the
impossible*. Sarah conceived long after it
seemed too late, because God keeps His
promises. Sounds good? It's because God
is good. So, spiritually, people connect
11:11 to *fulfilled promises* or *miraculous
timing* — that something long hoped for is
about to be realized.

In that day the Lord will reach out His
hand a second time to reclaim the
surviving remnant of His people. (Isaiah
11:11)

The meaning in this verse is
restoration and divine rescue. Those who
see 11:11 can sometimes take it as
reassurance that God is gathering and
restoring what was lost. Yes, God can do all
that, but He didn't say to tattoo it on
yourself. The *spirit* that encourages that
and constant cosmetic procedures is from
the evil marine kingdom. So, if you are
bearing their marks, it may be very difficult

to get release and deliverance from that *spirit*, or those *spirits*, depending on if there is a group of them. (There usually are.)

Folks, you can tattoo the entire Bible onto your body but if it is not in your heart and if God is not in you, then what have you done? Nothing.

When someone with a biblical worldview sees 11:11, they might take it as God whispering, "I'm still faithful. Stay aligned. I'm about to fulfill what I promised." But they may not. God said that the wicked are constantly looking for a sign. Isn't seeing 11:11 a sign? And then won't you continue to look for it?

A person could be saved, but by seeing a sign—11:11, they could be bounced right out of thinking of God to going into manifestation theories or into divination when they see 11:11. It depends on where and how they learned 11:11. Most people I believe it was in numerology or angel numbers. My Bible says, Hear O

Israel, the Lord Our God is one. It does not say that God is 11:11.

I am judging no one. I've had to repent of that myself. When humans hear the word, *angel*, we think it's divine or holy. In that way we can be sucked down wrong paths. The devil has angels--, fallen angels. He took a third of the stars with him when he fell like lightning from Heaven.

Repent if you need to, as well.

In New Age thought, **11:11** is seen as a *cosmic or energetic sign* rather than a message from God. Common beliefs include:

Portal or gateway number – 11:11 is thought to open a "spiritual portal" between dimensions or to higher consciousness. Some people meditate or make wishes at exactly 11:11, believing it's a time when intentions manifest more easily. Christians don't live by wish, we live by asking the Father in the Name of Jesus and by faith.

There are heavenly and divine portals and there are demonic and evil portals. People who don't know what they are doing may open up hell into their lives. (See my book: **Shut the Front Door: _Closing Evil Portals_** https://a.co/d/gH6hiXV

New Ageism sees 11:11 as an ascension code that signals that a person is awakening" or "vibrating" at a higher frequency, aligning with universal energies, spirit guides, or your "higher self." This is all divination; it is not of God, and it is evil. Spirit guides are demons.

New Agers see 11:11 as a synchronicity symbol. Followers of New Ageism interpret repeated numbers as "messages from the universe," angels, or one's own soul, confirming that you're on the right spiritual path.

In numerology, the number 11 is a "Master number." It represents enlightenment, and insight. Seeing it they think, represents amplified spiritual power or unity of physical and spiritual realms.

Biblically, 11 is the number for CHAOS. 11:11, then would be double chaos. Take heed, please.

Saints of God, from the Christian perspective, a crucial key difference is the SOURCE of the message. Whatever message you accept, whatever *spirits* are with or in or the source of the message come with that message. In Christianity, truth and revelation come from God, through the Holy Spirit and Scripture. A Word from God is a blessing and the blessings of the Lord make one rich and He adds no sorrow with it. So, no sneaky demons, devils, idol *gods* or evil *spirits* are attached to any message from God. The entities from the dark side bring sorrow, always. There is an initiation and evil covenants with agreeing with, using, or getting "help" from evil entities such as devils, demons, fallen angels, idols, idol *gods*, and powers from the dark kingdom.

New Ageism is pagan religion, repackaged over and again. In New Age belief, the "universe" or "energy" is often treated as an intelligent force that responds to your thoughts or vibrations, which replaces dependence on God with *self or cosmic alignment.*

That's why many Christian teachers caution that interpreting 11:11 through a *New Age* lens can blur the line between discernment and divination. It shifts focus from God's sovereignty to *energetic manifestation.* In other words, it downgrades God. We don't do that. Judas did that when he sold Jesus for the price of a slave. That didn't work out very well for Judas, did it?

I had not planned to talk about this, either--, but here we go. When people want fame, success, popularity and they resort to divination they corrupt every follower. What happens to the cult members who follow a cultish leader?

It is said – I don't know, I wasn't there, but it is said that "things" may be buried under the foundation of a building to bring those desired things such as fame, wealth, success. This smacks of Catholicism where certain of their "saints" are buried, and even upside down in a person's front yard when they want to sell a house. It is scandalously reported that some churches are built with dead things buried in the foundation or even under the very pulpit. I wasn't there, this is just what I have found in my studies and research. The person who did the burying, directed the burying and is benefitting from it is not getting power or even information from God, but from demonic sources.

Saints of God, try every spirit, and you shall know them by their fruit.

Beloved, believe not every spirit, but try the spirits whether they are of God: because many false prophets are gone out into the world.

Hereby know ye the Spirit of God: Every spirit that confesseth that Jesus Christ is come in the flesh is of God:

And every spirit that confesseth not that Jesus Christ is come in the flesh is not of

God: and this is that spirit of antichrist, whereof ye have heard that it should come; and even now already is it in the world.

Ye are of God, little children, and have overcome them: because greater is he that is in you, than he that is in the world.

They are of the world: therefore speak they of the world, and the world heareth them. (1 John 4:1-5)

Look For Patterns

When you see patterns, pay close attention. 11:11 is a pattern, you may say. Well, there are a lot of good scriptures in the Bible, not just certain ones that were numbered and chosen by men. The Bible was not written broken up into chapters and verses by God. Man did that. Superstition is not of God; that is also of man. Therefore, saying there is something special about a verse because of it's chapter and verse designation is of man, flesh, the soul, or the dark kingdom—not God.

A few years back I did a dive into the Bible where I looked for every verse that matched my birthday--, the month and day, in every Book of the Bible. It was only somewhat interesting because man made those chapter divisions and broke up the chapters into verses, not God.

From a scientific or skeptical perspective, 11:11 can be explained by pattern recognition: Humans naturally notice symmetry and repetition, so the brain pays extra attention to 11:11. Self-fulfilling prophecy is assisted by confirmation bias: Once you start noticing 11:11, you unconsciously look for it more often, reinforcing the idea that it's meaningful.

The world uses 11:11 in movies and songs to symbolize love, fate, or synchronicity. On social media, people post "11:11 make a wish" — a modern superstition meaning "wish time."

It is superstition.

So, if your "pastor" has this tattooed on him or herself, and especially if they did it after salvation, what is this *fruit*? Who are they serving? Is it a mix of "*gods*"? Is it a mix of *spirits*? Do you not know that those *spirits* are released and everyone who listens (repeatedly) to that person will suddenly or over time receive the *spirit* or *spirits* that he has? Especially if that pastor lays hands on you—it's a done deal. We can't know to the detail if our pastor is clean or not, unless we are in God and are faithful of heart, ourselves. We cannot know truly unless we are upright before the Lord ourselves.

If we are not clean before God anything can be sent to tell us anything. In that human way of self-fulfilling prophecy, we will see what was told to us. Absent the Holy Spirit, no matter how much we look or listen, we will unconsciously see what we want to see and only hear what we want to hear.

Howbeit when he, the Spirit of truth, is come, he will guide you into all truth: for he shall not speak of himself; but whatsoever he shall hear, *that* shall he speak: and he will shew you things to come. (John 16:13)

Dating & Other Relationships

You cannot be a spiritual disaster any more than you can be a physical disaster. But, you especially cannot be a spiritual disaster because it is the most dangerous and the most damaging thing you can be. No matter what comes up to you, it will hit, except for the Mercy of God. God can extend His Mercy wherever He wants, to both the saved and the unsaved, but outside of Mercy, you are outside of help.

If you are a walking magnet for trouble, unprotected spiritually, you are also putting whomever you are dating at risk as well.

In the natural, a spouse may snore. He has a C-PAP or a B-PAP machine, or other effective anti-snoring device, but he won't use it. The collateral damage is the non-snoring spouse can't sleep. They can't easily fall asleep or stay asleep. Worry sets in, especially when the snoring stops. This can wake a sleeping spouse up because they no longer hear the noise so they wake up to elbow the snorer who may have now moved into apnea and has stopped breathing completely.

Next thing you know, it's morning and you both get out of bed, exhausted, cranky. This is collateral damage. Your spouse doesn't even have a breathing problem, but night after night they have a problem because of you and your problem.

That's in the natural. Spiritually when you aren't saved, God's, spiritual, commune with God and are led by the Spirit of God, there will be no rest. There will be trouble. There will be affliction. There is no rest for the wicked. Those you led, encourage or talk into doing what you do and living like you live will be victims of collateral damage.

Collateral Damage Because of Association

This next section is not about being under judgment from God because of iniquity. It is about another layer being added, but also because of iniquity. When someone else close to you is being fired upon by evil arrows. And you just happen to be with them, friends with them, dating them, or in some other type of alliance or association or connection with them you are in line for collateral damage. No, I'm not trying to make anyone paranoid, just aware.

You can certainly tell by how many run-ins, near-misses, or hits that you've seen this in real life. When you look at your own life you can surely see many effects and then backtrace to find their causes. Now, from childhood I've endeavored to do right, I'm nearly a goody-two-shoes, but stuff just kept happening to me. It's generational, it's ancestral, but it is also right now. Not always right now because of sin, although I'm not perfect and we all have sinned and fallen short of the Glory of God. But in the immediate, in the now, stuff can be happening because of evil arrows that are fired just because the hearts of evil human persecutors are evil. Unfortunately, they can stick because of that same iniquity in our blood. That same blood that comes from our bloodline.

You know that kick a man when he's down thing? That's how enemy and witchcraft, evil human persecutor gang ups form. Monitory spirits are sent in to see where and how you can be attacked and the best day and way to do it. If you sense monitoring spirits, begin to pray then, blind them, get rid of them, and I even command them mute so they don't give their evil report. But it you look like a good target or an easy target, such as being a dry Christian or an unsaved heathen, altogether, then more than one altar from more than one source could try to fire on you.

Now you are a target for collateral damage because your great grandpa sinned and didn't repent or didn't ask to have the iniquity forgotten.

But it doesn't have to be grandpa— it could be you. it could be me who is the source of my own struggles and maybe even the source of afflictions or issues for another person entirely--, related or unrelated by blood.

The Lord had me to pray for those in my sphere who were, probably were, or were most likely suffering under collateral damage, like secondhand smoke or a Mary Jane high when that was never what they intended in the first place.

Years ago, I had dated and was seriously interested in a young man who was also working on a professional degree at the same time that I was. We had drifted apart and were each dating someone else. We loved the Lord, we talked Bible, and he was the most spiritual person that I knew at that time. I got two tickets to the Holy Land. The person who was to go with me did not. I called my most spiritual friend and asked if he wanted to go with? He said, of course. We went with a very large group of people from different churches. That is the only time I've been to the Holy Land; I don't know about him.

Okay, but you can't make this stuff up. We had known one another for a dozen or so years and we were still friends the first day or two there, but by the middle to the end of the trip, it seemed that he hated my guts. He had no kind words for me, was into comparison-*itis* mode. And he was grumpy with me about money. He had decided that I had more money than he did or that I made more money than he did. What did that have to do with the Holy

Land? What did that have to do with anything at all?

We had said that I'd take the still photos, and he'd take the videos. To this day, I've seen no videos of that trip. Not only that, he met a girl with one of he other congregations on this same Holy Land trip who was a stripper. Yes, on a Holy Land trip. You may be asking how is this collateral damage? Well certain negative events happened in my life that matched his. I believe I was the target and he was collateral damage. Both of us could have been the target for all I know.

At any rate, fast forward to just five years ago when I finally realized what happened to me 20 years or more ago in the Holy Land, **ALSO** happened to him. There was a person on this trip who had told me about it in the first place. He was a leader, he was there with his wife, and in his own group, but he was livid that I was there and with my friend, a male. How could I? he wanted to know. Didn't I know how this looked? I thought little of it because it didn't look any kind of way. We weren't dating, we weren't in sin, we weren't sleeping together. Our whole focus was on God, and I had fasted so long for this trip that I was downright skinny. I dismissed this "leader's" tirade and went on with participating in, learning about and enjoying the Holy Land, even though my longtime friend had turned on me. Up until that time, in nearly a dozen years, we had never spoken a cross or harsh word to one another.

Now my saved friend, who is in God has the responsibility to know if he has been hit by evil arrows or a spiritual spell. I have the same responsibility, however but were it not for me, he may not have been an object of the curse that this obvious to me now, witch, but a leader to the crowd had dispensed in our direction. Further, were it not for either of us not being prayed up, the arrows wouldn't have hit. Had it not been for our own spiritual foundations that curses could not have hit. But, saints of

God, had we not been fasted and as prayerful or worshipful as we were, it could have been worse.

But as I look, I see that what happened to me also happened to him. Collateral damage, as if a witch cares, they don't.

Men do not despise a thief, if he steal to satisfy his soul when he is hungry; But if he be found, he shall restore sevenfold; he shall give all the substance of his house. (Proverbs 6:30-31)

I want you to consider if you lost a friend or a relationship, was it due to collateral damage where you were the target but your spouse, friend, or associate also became a victim. A victim to witchcraft is why I am asking this.

Pray to the Lord and ask that He show you. He will. Now that thief who stole time and success and prosperity from both of us is finally caught and he must repay sevenfold, even if it means that he loses all of the substance of his house. It doesn't mean that you will get that friend or relationship back, but God is able to restore both of you to wholeness in your current relationship or in a new relationship if that particular one cannot be resurrected because of time having passed and other people now involved.

Witchcraft Damage

Somebody's significant other is a witch but you're dating their cheating boyfriend who is, or believes he is a non-witch. Blind or otherwise, because of the cheating, the witch gets angry at you, and they want revenge. They may be firing on you because you are "with" their boyfriend or girlfriend when you didn't even know they were married to, dating, or involved with anyone else. Yes, the person you are seeing lied to you, by omission if you never asked. But you should have asked. Right?

A scorned spouse can be very vengeful, and vengeance by man is not easily, if ever, satisfied? It is not worth it, people.

In this case you have real problems because if you are sleeping with a person who sleeps with and or is married to a witch. Therefore, they are a witch, unless they stop the association and renounce witchcraft. First of all, you are fornicating. God said don't do that—mostly to protect us, I'm sure. But if you are sleeping with a witch, you are being or have been initiated.

Oh? Into what?

Witchcraft.

This isn't really collateral damage, but it may be damage anyway. You may say you didn't know they were a witch, and you didn't know. And maybe you weren't even fornicating, maybe you were just friends. Or maybe you were having legal sex because you married the person, but their ex is still soul-tied and obsessed with them. For that reason, you may be receiving witchcraft arrow fire. It doesn't even have to be an ex; it could just be someone obsessed with them. It could be someone obsessed with you, in a good or a bad way.

That witch may not even be alone, they may be in a coven or just have "friends" who will agree with them in soulish, evil and diabolical prayers and incantations. All that is witchcraft. That is unfortunately a real thing.

Witchcraft arrows can be fired at a house against one person who lives there, but it may hit more than that one person. It may hit all in the house. Of course, you need to know the signs of witchcraft attack to know it there was a hit. That is collateral damage. If witchcraft is fired at a business, then the intent is to impact or destroy that business. However, for the people who work there will be collateral damage if that business suddenly has to close.

Also, be careful of those who are constant or perpetual victims. You know, those people who are your friends, but you are ever solving problems for them because this happened, that happened, or someone is always after them or doing something to them. They really may be victims; all that may be true. They may be under witchcraft attack and you decide to, in your flesh, make it all better for them. The Name of the Lord is a strong tower; the righteous run in and they are saved. The LORD is the high tower, not humans. When people need Jesus, we must lead them to Jesus and not to just ourselves.

The problem is in your flesh. Now, if you are sent by God and you go in the Spirit with the intention to heal, help, pray for, intercede for, then there is no problem. But when you go, without God's consent, whether it is a constant plight or not, but especially if it is, you may very well fall into the pit where they are.

Not as an excuse but when the Holy Land incident happened witchcraft was not anything I thought about or did anything about. We were so excited about the Bible, the Word of God and revelation of that Word. At that time, we considered witchcraft as something that if you didn't think about it or show fear about it then it didn't exist. That was really stupid and near-sighted of us because not only did it exist, but it is also talked about all through the Bible.

Based on the original Hebrew and Greek and standard English translations, such as KJV, NIV, and ESV, combined references the following was found: Witch Witchcraft or Witches: about 15–20 mentions total. Divination / Soothsaying / Fortune-telling: around 25–30 times. Sorcery / Sorcerers / Sorceress: about 15–20 times. Magic, magicians, enchantments and spells: roughly 25–30 times. Overall "occult or mystical arts" references, including necromancy, familiar *spirits,* astrology, etcetera were mentioned more than 70 times across both Testaments.

So, depending on translation there are **70–90 total passages** that explicitly address witchcraft, divination, sorcery, or related practices. Let us not read the Bible focusing just on the parts we like and skip inconvenient truths.

As A Parent

As a parent you will see patterns if you don't spiritually change your foundation and your life, your children will have the same life that you either loved or hated.

As a parent you have a mini-me, or more than one mini-me. Therefore, you should take with extreme seriousness everything you do and everything you have done. Deal with the sin and repent for it and the iniquity of it for sins you have already committed, else the fallout may fall on your mini-me or one of them, if you have more than one.

Then you have to take very seriously present day and future choices because when you sin, you sin for the entire family. You sin for the entire bloodline.

Concerning yourself with what it looks like to the neighborhood or other spectators is not the real measure. Believing you hid it because no one found out, is also not the marker. What did you do spiritually when you committed that sin in the natural? This works two ways, we are not saved by works, but doing a good work is attributed in your "good column" if God is keeping score. Good works are judged in the Bema Judgment. Whether or not you are saved is not judged there. The Bema Throne Judgment is the judging of the saved. Your works will be looked at as whether they are hay, wood, or stubble. In other words, do they burn?

So that is considered. However, what you did spiritually unless it is repented of and forgiven and expunged by God--, it will last for generations, and possibly forever in a bloodline. That could be damage to your future generations, and they could be blindsided by something they didn't even do, just as you may have already found out that an ancestor or some ancestors, at some time already sinned for you, leaving this iniquity. And you may have found out that iniquity left afflictions such as barrenness, poverty, madness, diseases, and worse.

The Most

The most collateral damage comes from people you know and spend time with. The absolute most is from the people that you are related to.

There can be an iniquity sandwich waiting to be shoved down your throat by the folks who gave birth to you. Those who gave you your smarts, cuteness, and feed you everyday --, what *spirits* are they harboring, what are they hiding? Do they even know? What are they spiritually doing nothing about? Whatever that is, it is lingering and it is waiting for you.

Even though vengeance is the Lord's, the iniquity is waiting with vengeance. Like your cell phone maker loves to brag about the next generation of their product, the next generation should be new and improved, but it will be bigger and badder. Unless it is handled spiritually, then it can be bigger and better.

It is called spiritual mapping, It's like retrofitting, when you look to see what is happening in your family, or in yourself. What is the affliction? Once that is assessed, now you have to become a backtrack sleuth to find or figure out what was done in the previous generation that led to the current problem or affliction in yourself or your family. If it's brand-new sin, then it is yours, but we are talking about generational or ancestral iniquity. At the point of affliction, it is not a blame game, it is something that must be handled as you realize that the people who you are related to have the most affect—good or bad, in your life, absent Jesus.

Therefore, the goal is to find the Lord and run into that High Tower and be saved and then be fully converted, do your warfare and ask the Lord to remove the iniquity in your bloodline.

'It don't take all that' saints – in some bloodlines it does. Thank God if it is not you and yours.

When It Is Your Fault

When it is your fault…if you are a walking disaster. Dare I say? A walking curse. There are times when we humans want someone to bail us out. There are times when people go *through*, and they don't seem to be coming out of their problems so they may try to find someone to latch onto so that person will bring them up or bring them out. We see this all the time as movie plots. A poor, broke or downtrodden person wants to meet and connect with a rich person, marry them or go into business with them so their condition in life can be changed and upgraded.

Well, this depends on how the person got into that position. If they are in trouble with God, if they are under judgement of God, then no amount of anything in the natural will fix that. It will take repentance and the favor of God turning back on them for things to change.

No man can undo what God has set in place. No demon, no devil. Only God can rescind His orders and place a man back in favor if he has fallen from the Grace of God.

In the natural, for example, if you are an artist or nail tech but you somehow develop an unsteady hand, what do you think the nails you polish will look like? So, you get your hand steady or correct whatever is the matter first so the people who come to you for manicures will look really nice instead of like they did their own nails, or worse, their child painted their nails for them.

Any of us may say that it is impossible to wait until some spiritual condition is cleared up before we return back to work. We have to work. Well, then repent to God quickly and do the work, prayers, fasting, warfare—whatever is needed so the state of your being doesn't negatively impact others. This may sound very altruistic, and it should be.

For example, if you have a cold, flue, or other, normally contagious respiratory issue, you do not go to work, right? Or are you one to go to work just because you feel better? Or you feel that you don't want to miss your hours, or you just don't care that you have a cold and the whole office could get it? Collateral damage is when you take your germs, disease, cold or whatever and give it to other people, who may not have ever known you had a cold because you masked the symptoms with meds. Some of your victims may be strangers, and you may walk away and never know they got sick for two weeks and suffered or lost time from work, or took it home to their entire family. Still, you may give the cold you got to people in your family or household. Collateral damage; they got hurt just because of being in association, connection with, or proximity to you.

There are people who can be carriers of certain contagious diseases who may not have the disease or any of its symptoms, but they can carry the disease to others. It's still their fault. This is why we use the utmost in hygiene when around others, especially if we are going to be preparing food for them, for example.

I went into a Chipotle, shortly after the time of the COVID shut down. You know it's a wide-open kitchen. I didn't see any of the workers in the kitchen, just the cashier and the people on the line. Suddenly three people, I suppose kitchen staff ran in from the back. They may have been on break or taking a smoke outside, who can say? None of them were wearing masks. But one of the people sneezed, sneezed, and then sneezed again. I left. I didn't go back there for more than two years after that incident.

I will not go to the place that sings over your ice cream as they make it. Do you have any idea how much "spray" comes out of any mouth when you talk? When you cough? When you sing? They are mixing your food; their heads are down, and they are might as well say, spitting all over your food.

No thanks.

I am leery of cooks in kitchens that I can't see. Are they tasting the food and putting the spoon back in the same pot? These people may be completely healthy, but it doesn't mean that their germs, their bacteria are compatible with your immune system. Why would you take up the spit of a stranger and eat it?

If we cannot be aware of collateral damage we may be causing in the natural, with things and people we can see, then it may be nearly impossible to understand this in a spiritual context. So, let's look at it this way:

Sneezing generates a short, violent burst of internal droplets being forced out of a person's lungs, creating lots of droplets, and an immediate spray. It can go as far as 8 meters away, lasting 26 minutes in the area. We most often can't see the spray, but it is there. Sometimes we do see it and it looks like a fine mist emanating from a person's mouth and shooting across the room. Immediately it seems to be "gone"; but it is not. That spray went up to 26 feet (almost 9 yards) away from the sneezer.

Coughing is similar, but the distance is up to three meters (10 feet) away, lasting up to 10 minutes in the environment. Folks, could this be where we get sayings like, 'I wouldn't touch it with a 10-foot pole'?

Singing can unleash a steady, continuous aerosol output, also one to three meters away that can accumulate indoors, lasting up to 30 minutes. This depends on ventilation, airflow and etcetera, but it still goes up to three meters away from the happy soul that's singing. (Not over my food; sorry.)

Talking aerosol is continuous, as long as the person is talking that can spread about a meter away, lasting up to 20 minutes in the room.

Breathing creates a quiet but persistent aerosol source that spreads invisibly up to six and a half feet (2m) away. It spreads invisibly, especially in closed rooms and lasts up to hours.

Sinning creates an invisible iniquity that spreads as far as it can and lasts up to 4 generations in a bloodline.

So even if we are just living, moving, breathing, and having our being, we affect our environment and others around us. If we decide to sin, then we impact things much differently, more dramatically, and in a more damaging way. Sin and its iniquity stays in the environment of your bloodline for a long time if not repented of, forgiven and the iniquity removed. Hiding it and trying to cover it up is what makes it last even longer. The longer it lasts the more people it could affect. I say that because a couple may have two kids. Their kids get married and they may end up with six or more grandchildren. Now the grandchildren all get married and they end up with 20 great grandchildren. More targets for spiritual fallout.

Saints of God, we can see sin, if we are near it. We may be able to hear it and detect it with other senses, however the iniquity that comes with it may not be visible right away, for generations, or at all. We can hear many bodily functions such as sneezing, coughing, singing, talking, and sometimes our own and other people's breathing. However, the spray that comes from them is usually invisible and lingers in the environment for a certain amount of time. That is like iniquity. We cannot see it until it afflicts either ourselves or another person. Either now, soon, or in another generation. It's the same as sometimes we cannot see the cold that got passed from

79

one person to another because they were a stranger on the subway or the plane and they went their way and you yours, but were you the cause of their new respiratory illness because you took yours on the plane or train--, out in public?

Simply put, your great, great grandpa got a bad cold with massive sneezes and 4 generations later you got a "cold" that was not really a cold but some spiritual affliction. But you never saw it coming. Your parents never saw it because it was invisible, just out there hovering, waiting to land. And it could be that the person it landed on had no spiritual immunity or defenses because of being a dry Christian or not saved at all. This is like collateral damage caused by a sinner.

Sin is sin. All sin is sin, but depending on the severity or the wickedness of a person's sin and the state of their heart afterward will iniquity be assessed. By wickedness, it can be understood that the sin that creates the most havoc or damage, the most destruction or losses is more wicked than one that only affects one or a few. Individual sin is bad enough, but sin that involves or compromises a family, a congregation, a city, a nation will be judged differently than the sins that do not affect many people or destinies. This is why pastors, teachers, prophets and the like will be judged differently than regular sit-on-the-pew people. The more authority one has, the more and stronger they can impact others.

Look at David's repentance, deep, sorrowful, long (Psalm 51). Pharoah, on the other hand—hardened heart, didn't repent. Surely Pharoah who thought he was right all along, is in hell, while David has a descendant on the Throne.

There is a way which seemeth right unto a man, but the end thereof are the ways of death. (Proverbs 14:12)

When You Have Done Nothing Wrong

When you know to do, and don't do anything, that will be accounted to you as sin. So, if you sinned and know you've sinned and you rebelliously choose not to repent and turn from your wicked ways, that is more sin over the sin already committed. That is more iniquity piling up to create spiritual collateral damage especially down your bloodline and among your associates and perhaps even extending to strangers.

Remember, it is sin to know what you ought to do and then not do it. (James 4:17 NLT)

But when you are experiencing blowback or fallout and it is not your fault then with all that is in you, run to God and He will help you as you cry for Mercy. Cry for Mercy because iniquity in your bloodline may have found you. Cry for Mercy because evil from a fake friend or stranger may have found you.

When you have become so shocked, suddenly oppressed or so selfish that you only are concerned about your survival, well-being or comfort, then it is as though you have done nothing. Sin can be inflicted upon a person and it could be as a sudden terror that shocks a person. In that shock they may do nothing or feel they don't know what to do. If you feel that you are stuck, that could be a result of witchcraft attack so you don't even do what you know to do, or forget what you know to do, or what you would normally do in a given situation. When you suspect witchcraft attack, go into spiritual warfare. Start by repenting to God. You may have done nothing wrong, but something in you may be allowing the attack.

Next, ask for Mercy.

Now, send back evil arrows. If you don't know what kind of arrows to send back, just say, "Every evil arrow"—start there. (Prayer on Warfare Prayer Channel. https://www.youtube.com/watch?v=uEr8sls5sJ4&t=9137s

Book transcription: https://a.co/d/hzSTYC2) From praying that way, you may experience some relief and then the Holy Spirit will lead you into what and how to pray next to get you extricated from whatever net or trap has been set for you.

Godly Sorrow

The following was the real impetus for this book: After realization and repenting because you, yourself are afflicted or have been going through. After doing your own spiritual warfare and seeking deliverance, you may have then (quickly or slowly) realized that whatever happened to you also happened to another person that you are or were connected to in some way. We see on soap operas and in the movies all the time that a person may feel so guilty because of what befell another character in the storyline. Godly sorrow is better than guilt. Guilt won't tell you to get up and repent and repay or make retribution or pray deliverance for anyone that you also hurt or anyone who got hurt because of your actions or spiritual state. By spiritual state, I mean if a person is full of sin and iniquity and is a spiritual target either by their own wrongdoings and/or generational iniquity, then they are dangerous to others by relationship, connection, and by proximity to your vicinity.

Yes, pray for all the souls on the airplane you are about to board, that today is not a day for anyone's demise, in the Name of Jesus.

Now, back to a family member, friend, or someone you were associated with you who has gone through the exact or near-exact thing that you have been going through. For instance, if you've gone into captivity, so have they, even if you have lost contact with them. If you've been in captivity, they have most likely also. Maybe they've gotten deliverance, maybe they haven't. if they have been delivered, but haven't come back to get you, by prayer in the spiritual realm, that doesn't mean that you don't go back to get them out of spiritual captivity.

Whether they came back to get you or not, once you have figured this thing out, now that you understand what happened spiritually, you should tell them, warn them and perhaps you two can pray together. If you know and say nothing, that is the same as not warning them. Remember the role of the watchman. If the two of you are out of touch and you have no way of telling them, then be sure you pray for their deliverance.

The sword, the spell, the curse, the evil may have already happened and there was no watchman who gave prior notice, but when deliverance has come, let it be announced and let the Lord be mighty and let the Lord be magnified. Amen.

This is one another ministry, whether they know it or not. Whether they are related to you or not. You have authority here to pray for them if you are related to them. You have authority because you were involved in their captivity in the first place. Especially if you feel it was your attack that trapped them also, or it was because of their relationship with you that some irrational evil human persecutor pursued them and overtook them. Regarding my Holy Land friend, perhaps he never would have come under the scope of the "evil leader" if he had not gone with me on the Jerusalem tour. Perhaps he would have? Perhaps some other persecutor would have gotten him? Perhaps not. Whether is was destiny for his destiny to be affected or ruined is not the question: If you have authority to pray for a person and the spiritual wherewithal and connection to the Holy Spirit to bring them out of captivity, then you do it.

If they were never captive, or never knew it, then the prayers won't hurt them.

And when you were rescued, did you have the awareness to ask if those who were captive with you could also come out? Friends? Family? Strangers, or those who were not strong enough or aware enough to do that yet?

Go back now and ask the Lord to rescue them. Go into the Courts of Heaven and plead this case.

The same anointing, the same power that delivered you can also deliver them.

Micah 4:6 speaks of a return from captivity. God can deliver more than just one, He can deliver all. Did he not bring millions across the Red Sea on dry land? Did he not return Israel's captivity from Babylon, more than once? So, after your own deliverance, I exhort you, Dear Reader, go back and get your brother. Go back for your family, go back for your friends and loved ones. All who want to come out when you call to them, will. No matter how you see yourself--, even if you see yourself as small or weak, it is the anointing that breaks the yokes. Because of the anointing that sets you free can also set others free.

In Christ, we all have both the Grace and responsibility for deliverance; it is the children's bread.

In that day," declares the Lord,

"I will gather the lame;
I will assemble the exiles
and those I have brought to grief.
I will make the lame my remnant,
those driven away a strong nation.
The Lord will rule over them in Mount
Zion
from that day and forever.
As for you, watchtower of the flock,
stronghold of Daughter Zion,
the former dominion will be restored to
you;
kingship will come to Daughter
Jerusalem."

Why do you now cry aloud—
have you no king?
Has your rule perished,
that pain seizes you like that of a
woman in labor?
Writhe in agony, Daughter Zion,
like a woman in labor,
for now you must leave the city
to camp in the open field.
You will go to Babylon;
there you will be rescued.

There the Lord will redeem you
out of the hand of your enemies.

But now many nations
are gathered against you.
They say, "Let her be defiled,
let our eyes gloat over Zion!"
But they do not know
the thoughts of the Lord;
they do not understand his plan,
that he has gathered them like sheaves
to the threshing floor.
"Rise and thresh, Daughter Zion,
for I will give you horns of iron;
I will give you hooves of bronze,
and you will break to pieces many
nations."
You will devote their ill-gotten gains to
the Lord,
their wealth to the Lord of all the earth.
(Micah 4:6-13)

Pray for One Another

Lord, have Mercy on me, a sinner. If I am none of Yours, give me a repentant heart and a Godly sorrow for my sins, and make me one of Yours, in the Name of Jesus.

Lord, fill me with Your spirit, the Holy Spirit of God.

Holy Spirit, help me in these prayers, in the Name of Jesus.

Lord, I've come to repent of causing collateral damage in the life, soul, heart, body, ministry or marriage or destiny of anyone, in the Name of Jesus.

Lord, I come to the Throne of Grace to receive Grace and Mercy. You said we could come boldly.

In the presence of the Blood of Jesus, I ask, Father, if there is an accusation up against me by anyone, any entity, let them bring forth their evidence, documents and accusations at this time.

Jesus Christ is my Advocate, thank You, Lord.

…. Yes, I am guilty, and my defense is the Blood of Jesus. Thank You, Lord. I am redeemed from every curse, every accusation, every issue, by the Blood of Jesus.

Lord, have Mercy on me if I am under divine judgement. I repent. I repent for the sins of my parents and my ancestors, going all the way back to Adam and Eve, in the Name of Jesus.

Lord, forgive all our iniquity, in the Name of Jesus.

I break every evil covenant, and I repent of, renounce and denounce the sin that caused it, in the Name of Jesus. Lord, forgive me.

I break every evil covenant in place in my bloodline, and I repent of, renounce and denounce the sin that caused it, in the Name of Jesus.

I break and dismantle every evil spell, curse, incantation, divination, enchantment by any witch, wizard, warlock, sorcerer, that is up against me, in the Name of Jesus.

Lord, forgive me for any evil or negative spiritual thing that has come up to me, upon me, or attached to me that has affected anyone else whatsoever, in the Name of Jesus.

Lord, forgive me for quenching the Holy Spirit, for grieving or ignoring the Holy Spirit, in the Name of Jesus.

Lord, forgive me for not using discernment and not using it in a timely way, in the Name of Jesus.

Lord, forgive me for straight up ignorance when I didn't even know anything spiritual was happening around me, in the Name of Jesus.

Forgive me, Father for being a dry Christian, not being prayed up, in the Name of Jesus.

Father, forgive me for not practicing the disciplines of the faith on a regular basis, in the Name of Jesus.

Because of the Blood of Jesus, I declare that I am curse-less; no evil can attach to me. I am in Christ, and the devil has nothing in Christ, Amen.

Father, forgive me for evil alliances, wrong connections, being in wrong places with wrong people, in the Name of Jesus.

Forgive me for putting myself ignorantly or rebelliously in harm's way, in the Name of Jesus.

Lord, forgive me of all sin, especially sins of immorality, sexual sins, fornication, adultery, in the Name of Jesus.

Lord, if I have ever slept with a witch, I repent with Godly sorrow and I ask You to break any and every initiation into witchcraft, whether knowingly or unknowingly, whether consciously or unconsciously, whether willingly or whether I was forced, in the Name of Jesus.

Father, break every spell of bewitchment on me, in the Name of Jesus.

Forgive me, Lord if I knowingly or unknowing induced anyone to sin, in the Name of Jesus.

Forgive me if I have caused any man to stumble or fall, in the Name of Jesus.

Forgive me, Lord, if I have unknowingly or knowingly hurt anyone myself by blind witchcraft or any other way, in the Name of Jesus.

Lord, reverse my captivity so that I am free to do, be, move and have being, in the Name of Jesus.

Lord, do not leave my soul in hell. Do not suffer your darling… in the Name of Jesus.

…

I am set free, in the Name of Jesus.

And, now I call out my brother --, my sister who has been in affliction or in sorrow out of captivity, in the Name of Jesus.

Lord, let the same anointing, the same power, the same Mercy and Grace that delivered me, also deliver my brother / sister, (insert their name here), in the Name of Jesus.

Lord, forgive me and may they also forgive me if I was the cause of collateral spiritual damage coming upon them, in the Name of Jesus.

____, ____, come out, in the Name of Jesus. (repeat as led by the Holy Spirit.

Lord, you delivered me from the bear, the lion, You brought me out of the pit, out of the miry clay. You set my feet on a large place, and now I ask, deliver my brother, deliver my sister, deliver anyone who desires deliverance, who needs deliverance who You will, in the Name of Jesus.

Lord, bring out of captivity anyone who is in lockdown due to my own negligence, sin, disobedience, rebellion, iniquity, in the Name of Jesus.

Lord, anyone who went into captivity because of me, or at the same time I did just by association or alliance, bring them out as well.

Father, have your angels search the land of the living and the dead and find every piece and part of their soul and bring them out, in the Name of Jesus.

(You will find the blueprint and more than 100 prayer points in the book, **Get Out of Captivity** https://a.co/d/87Nz1YC. Also I've written other books about Captivity and breaking free.) Also, **Caged Life** and **WTH? Get Me Out of This Hell.**

Redeem the Time

Now, ask the Lord to redeem the time for both yourself and for them—for anyone who was hurt of lost time, progress or momentum as a result of collateral damage because of your destruction, being caught up in your wake. Of course if you've been fully redeemed, praise God, but the same anointing that delivered you will also deliver them. In this way you are praying for yourself as you pray for them. Just as when someone is being prayed for in a prophetic service you tap into that anointing and receive while the Spirit is moving.

We do see some Biblical examples of redemption after damage. Even when innocent people suffered, God often brought restoration:

After the flood, God promised never to destroy all life again (Genesis 9:11). After David's plague, God instructed him to build an altar, thus, turning judgment into reconciliation (2 Samuel 24:25).

Jesus healed those hurt by sin, showing that Grace can follow destruction. Jesus did not just offer healing, He offered wholeness. And we, too should endeavor to leave people better than we found them. Amen.

The Bible's examples remind us that the ripple effects of human choices often reach far beyond the people who made them, sometimes generations later. Even unintended harm still leaves real wounds, and yet, again and again, Scripture shows that God can redeem the aftermath of what was lost or broken.

Ask yourself: "Whose pain today might be the echo of my decision, my choice, my act, my sin? And now, whose healing might begin because of mine?"

Do not be deceived: God is not mocked, for whatever one sows, that will he also reap. (Galatians 6:7 ESV)

God shows Mercy amid fallout.

The Lord is compassionate and gracious, slow to anger, abounding in love. He will not always accuse, nor will he harbor his anger forever; he does not treat us as our sins deserve or repay us according to our iniquities. (Psalm 103:8-10 NIV)

Our redemption is through Christ Jesus.

As he went along, he saw a man blind from birth. His disciples asked him, "Rabbi, who sinned, this man or his parents, that he was born blind?" Jesus replied, "Neither this man nor his parents sinned... but this happened so that the works of God might be displayed in him. (John 9:1-3 NIV)

Even where there has been collateral damage, whether from sin, pride, or pain, God's Grace can still write the final line.

The Bible presents collateral damage as part of a moral tension between justice and mercy. Sometimes, harm to others reveals the corporate nature of sin. One person's rebellion can ripple through families and nations.

Ezekiel and Jeremiah emphasized that God takes no pleasure in the death of the wicked. This is why we don't over celebrate when God defeats our enemies. We make our boast in the Lord, not in ourselves or our own power. Nor do we mock them or rail against dignities. We make our boast in the Lord with sobriety toward the wicked, even when they finally fall. Sometimes our deliverance is delayed until we get a right heart about just that. If you are going to gloat and act a fool and mock and deride when your enemies fall, God may just be waiting for you to get an sober understanding of what is happening spiritually before He takes another step toward your deliverance.

This is not your grade school playground; this is serious, with lasting reverberations.

Any man's death diminishes me, because I am involved in Mankind. (John Donne).

But chiefly them that walk after the flesh in the lust of uncleanness, and despise government. Presumptuous are they, selfwilled, they are not afraid to speak evil of dignities.(2 Peter 2:10)

Jesus' teachings reframe this by urging compassion and forgiveness, warning that sin and hardness of heart still produce unintended harm (Matthew 5–7, Luke 13:1–5).

Collateral damage: Even unintended harm still leaves real wounds, and yet, again and again, Scripture shows that God can redeem the aftermath of what was lost or broken.

Restore & Recompense

And I will restore to you the years that
the locust hath eaten. (Joel 2:25)

Lord, You are My Shepherd.

The LORD is my shepherd, I lack nothing.

He makes me lie down in green pastures,
He leads me beside quiet waters,

He refreshes my soul.

He guides me along the right paths for His
Name's sake.

Even though I walk through the darkest
valley, I will fear no evil, for You are with
me, Your Rod and Your Staff, they comfort
me.

You prepare a table before me in the
presence of my enemies. You anoint my
head with oil; my cup overflows.

Surely Your goodness and Love will follow me all the days of my life, and I will dwell in the house of the LORD, forever.

Prayer used from: https://thegracefulchapter.com/use-psalm-23-as-a-prayer/

Lord, recompense all the people who were hurt, damaged, disappointed for all their losses and pain that I may have affected while I was under a curse, in the Name of Jesus.

Recompense them for losses, hurts, pain, disappointments because I was not in the right place at the right time, in Jesus' Name.

Recompense them for any suffering whatsoever because of my missteps, misdeeds, in the Name of Jesus.
Lord, forgive me, in the Name of Jesus.

Redeeming the time, because the days are evil. Wherefore be ye not unwise, but understanding what the will of the Lord is. (Ephesians 5:16-17)

AMEN

Prayerbooks by this author

While most books by this author have prayer points either throughout the book or at the end, there are some books that are only prayers. You just open up the book and pray.

Prayers Against Barrenness: *For Success in Business and Life*

Fruit of the Womb: *Prayers Against Barrenness*

Beauty Curses, *Warfare Prayers Against*
https://a.co/d/5Xlc20M

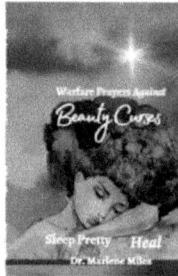

Courts of Marriage: Prayers for Marriage in the Courts of Heaven *(prayerbook)*
https://a.co/d/cNAdgAq

Courtroom Warfare @ Midnight

(prayerbook) https://a.co/d/5fc7Qdp

Demonic Cobwebs *(prayerbook)*

https://a.co/d/fp9Oa2H

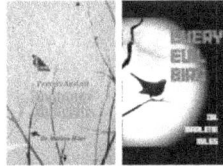

Every Evil Bird https://a.co/d/hF1kh1O

Gates of Thanksgiving

Spirits of Death, Hell & the Grave, Pass Over Me and My House

Throne of Grace: Courtroom Prayer

Warfare Prayer Against Poverty

https://a.co/d/bZ611Yu

Other books by this author

AK: The Adventures of the Agape Kid

Already Married in the Spirit: *Why You May Not Be Married in the Natural*

AMONG SOME THIEVES
https://a.co/d/dkYT4ZV

Ancestral Powers

Anti-Marriage, *The Spirit of*

Backstabbers https://a.co/d/gi8iBxf

Barrenness, *Prayers Against*
https://a.co/d/feUltIs

Battlefield of Marriage, *The*

Beware of the Dog: Prayers Against Dogs in the Dream.

Bless Your Food: *Let the Dining Table be Undefiled*

Blindsided: *Has the Old Man Bewitched You?* https://a.co/d/5O2fLLR

Break Free from Collective Captivity

Broken Spirits & Dry Bones

By Means of a Whorish Father

Caged Life: Get Out Alive!

https://a.co/d/bwPbksX

Casting Down Imaginations

Churchzilla, The Wanna-Be, Supposed-to-be Bride of Christ

Demonic Cobwebs (prayerbook)

Demonic Time Bombs

Demons Hate Questions

Devil Loves Trauma, *The*

Devil Weapons: Unforgiveness, Bitterness,…

The Devourers: Thieves of Darkness 2

Do Not Swear by the Moon

Don't Refuse Me, Lord (4 book series)

https://a.co/d/idP34LG

Dream Defilement

The Emptiers: *Thieves of Darkness, 1*
https://a.co/d/5I4n5mc

Evil Touch

Failed Assignment

Fantasy Spirit Spouse
https://a.co/d/hW7oYbX

FAT Demons (The): *Breaking Demonic Curses* https://a.co/d/4kP8wV1

The Fold (5-book series)

- The Fold (Book 1)
- Name Your Seed (Book 2)
- The Poor Attitudes of Money (3)
- Do Not Orphan Your Seed (4)
- For the Sake of the Gospel (5)
- My Sowing Journal

Gang Ups: Touch Not God's Anointed

Getting Rid of Evil Spiritual Food

https://a.co/d/i2L3WYQ

got HEALING? Verses for Life

got LOVE? Verses for Life

got HOPE? Verses for Life

got money? https://a.co/d/g2av41N

Has   My   Soul   Been   Sold?
https://a.co/d/dyB8hhA

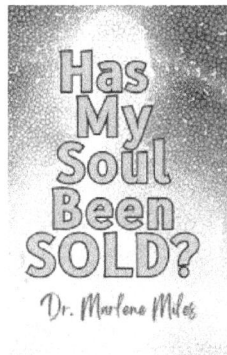

Here Come the Horns: *Skilled to Destroy*
https://a.co/d/cZiNnkP

Hidden Sins: Hidden Iniquity

https://a.co/d/4Mth0wa

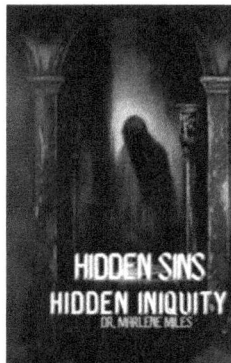

How to Dental Assist

How to Dental Assist2: Be Productive, Not Wasteful

How to STOP Being a Blind Witch or Warlock

I Take It Back

Legacy

Let Me Have A Dollar's Worth
https://a.co/d/h8F8XgE

Level the Playing Field

Living for the NOW of God

Lose My Location
https://a.co/d/crD6mV9

Love Breaks Your Heart

Made Perfect In Love

Mammon https://a.co/d/29yhMG7

Man Safari, *The*

Marriage Ed. Rules of Engagement & Marriage

Made Perfect in Love

Money Hunters: Beware of Those

Money on the Altar https://a.co/d/4EqJ2Nr

Mulberry Tree, *The*
https://a.co/d/9nR9rRb

Motherboard (The)~ *Soul Prosperity Series*

Name Your Seed

Occupy: *Until I Return*
https://a.co/d/bZ7ztUy

Plantation Souls

Players Gonna Play

Portals: Shut the Front Door: Prayers to Close Evil Portals.

Power Money: Nine Times the Tithe

https://a.co/d/gRt41gy

The Power to Get Wealth
https://a.co/d/e4ub4Ov

Powers Above

The Robe, Part 1, The Lessons of Joseph

The Robe, Part II, The Lessons of Joseph

Seasons of Grief

Seasons of Waiting

Seasons of War

Second Marriage, Third~~, *Any Marriage*

https://a.co/d/6m6GN4N

Seducing Spirits: Idolatry & Whoredoms

https://a.co/d/4Jq4WEs

Shut the Front Door: *Prayers to Close Portals* https://a.co/d/cH4TWJj

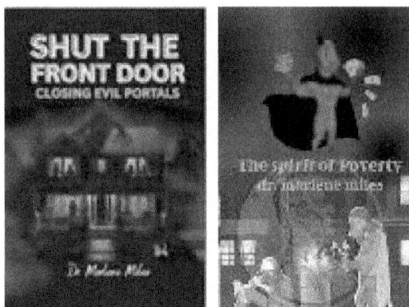

Sift You Like Wheat

Six Men Short: What Has Happened to all the Men?

SLAVE

Sleep Afflictions & Really Bad Dreams
https://a.co/d/f8sDmgv

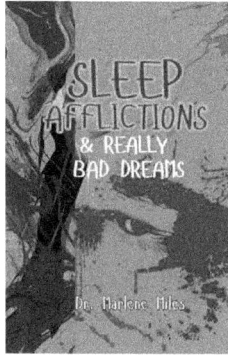

Soul Prosperity soul prosperity series 3

https://a.co/d/5p8YvCN

Souls Captivity soul prosperity series 2

The Spirit of Anti-Marriage

The Spirit of Poverty
https://a.co/d/abV2o2e

Spiritual Thieves https://a.co/d/eqPPz33

StarStruck- Triangular Power series.

SUNBLOCK- Triangular Power series.

The Swallowers: *Thieves of Darkness,* 3

Take It Back

This Is NOT That: How to Keep Demons from Coming at You

Time Is of the Essence

Too Many Wives: *Why You Have Lady Problems*

Tormenting Spirits
https://a.co/d/dAogEJf

Toxic Souls

Triangular Power *(series),* Powers Above, SUNBLOCK, Do Not Swear by the Moon, STARSTRUCK

Unbreak My Heart: *Don't Let Me Die*

Uncontested Doom

Unguarded Hours, *The*

Unseen Life, *The* (forthcoming)

Upgrade: How to Get Out of Survival Mode Toxic Souls (Book 2 of series) , Legacy (Book 3 of series)

The Wasters: *Thieves of Darkness,* Bk 2
https://a.co/d/bUvI9Jo

What Have You to Declare? What Do You Have With You from Where You've Been?

When I Was A Child, *I Prayed As a Child*

When the Devourer is Rebuked

https://a.co/d/1HVv8oq

WTH? Get Me Out of This Hell
https://a.co/d/a7WBGJh

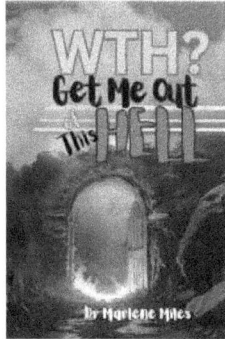

The Wilderness Romance *(series)* This series is about conducting a Godly relationship and marriage with someone who is a Wilderness person. It is about how to recognize it and navigate through it. These books are about how not to get caught up in such.

- *The Social Wilderness*
- *The Sexual Wilderness*
- *The Spiritual Wilderness*

Other Series

The Fold (a series on Godly finances)
https://a.co/d/4hz3unj

Soul Prosperity Series https://a.co/d/bz2M42q

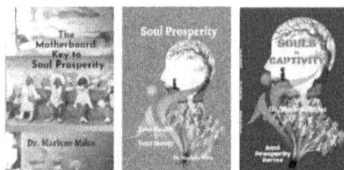

Spirit Spouse books

https://a.co/d/9VehDSo

https://a.co/d/97sKOwm

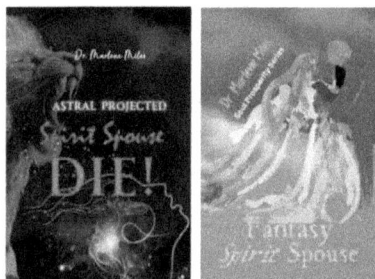

Battlefield of Marriage, The

https://a.co/d/eUDzizO

Players Gonna Play

https://a.co/d/2hzGw3N

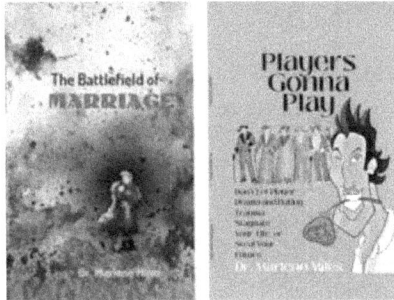

Sent Spirit Spouse (can someone send you a spirit spouse? This book is not yet released.)

Matters of the Heart, Made Perfect in Love https://a.co/d/70MQW3O , Love Breaks Your Heart https://a.co/d/4KvuQLZ, Unbreak My Heart https://a.co/d/84ceZ6M Broken Spirits & Dry Bones https://a.co/d/e6iedNP

Thieves of Darkness series

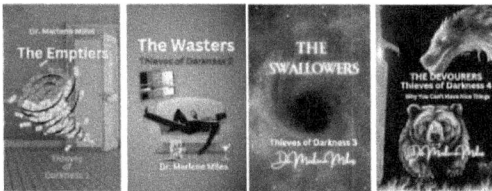

The Emptiers https://a.co/d/heio0dO

The Wasters https://a.co/d/5TG1iNQ

The Swallowers https://a.co/d/1jWhM6G

The Devourers: Why We Can't Have Nice Things https://a.co/d/87Tejbf

Spiritual Thieves

Triangular Powers https://a.co/d/aUCjAWC

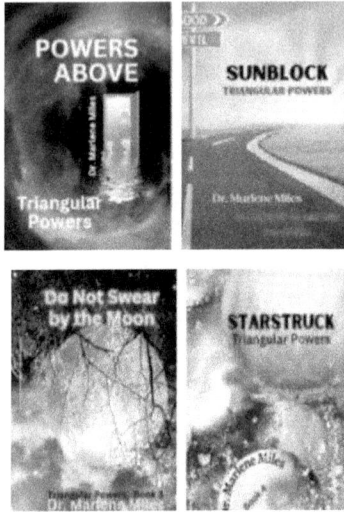

Upgrade (series) *How to Get Out of Survival Mode* https://a.co/d/aTERhXO

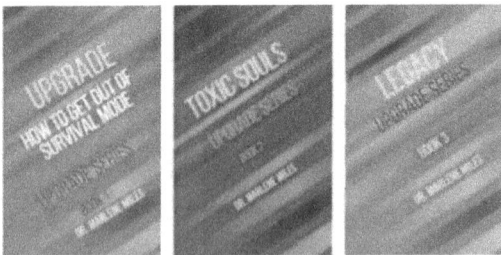

www.ingramcontent.com/pod-product-compliance
Lightning Source LLC
LaVergne TN
LVHW051419080426
835508LV00022B/3159